A Beginner's Guide
to
Choosing and Planting Summer Flowers

In containers, window boxes and
hanging baskets

Compiled and Photographed
by
Penelope Murray

with
Kelly McSorley

ISBN: 978-1-5262-0326-7

PublishNation
www.publishnation.co.uk

For Taffy and Herman
Wishing them all the joy and happiness
in gardens as I have always found

With very many thanks to Kelly Mc,
Kelly Fitz, and especially to Darren

CONTENTS

https://beginnergardeners.wixsite.com/beginnergardeners

Introduction

My young neighbours James and Lisa said to me, "If I don't know the names of flowers how can I look them up to see when, where and how to grow them".

This simple remark inspired me to compile a book listing flowers under their colours so that beginner gardeners are able to choose whatever they would like to have in their gardens in the summer months, in containers, hanging baskets and window boxes, with a small outlay and little maintenance required.

I have included some thirty plants in this book which should be available in your local garden centre from April through to the end of June. Underneath each photograph I have listed a few helpful details about the shapes of the plants, where it is advisable to plant them, the height they will grow to and the other colours the plant may also be found in.

On the following page I have explained the Lifespan of Plants, i.e. annuals, perennials and evergreens.

There is then a section and accompanying photographs to show you how to plant in pots and containers, window boxes and hanging baskets, followed by a small section and photographs of everyday herbs grown in pots.

The Lifespan of Plants

Annuals

These are plants which germinate, flower and die within a year. When you have chosen annuals in your local garden centre which are in tiny forms (not flowering already) you should plant them out in your pots and containers, window boxes or hanging baskets as soon as you get them home. When the plants have died at the end of the summer you should throw them away.

A few plants included here may be both annuals and perennials. In which case you can either throw them away or keep them in the container and look after them until next spring. Personally, I find Geraniums are the most likely to survive from one year to the next.

Perennials

These are plants which will live for several years and grow bigger each year. In gardens centres they will mostly be sold in individual pots. After they have flowered during the summer months they will die back but their roots will remain under the soil dormant during the winter months. In the spring they will produce new shoots and flower again in the summer. In a flower bed they should be planted with plenty of space around them to allow for their growth.

Evergreens

These plants will live for several years and while their flowers may die they will not shed their leaves during the years. These plants also need to be grown with some space around them to allow for their growth.

Compost

Compost is the 'soil' used to grow plants in pots and containers, window boxes and hanging baskets.

MULTI-PURPOSE COMPOST

I recommend this compost for plants that will be in containers, window boxes and hanging baskets for only a few months during one summer as it is a specially formulated compost which provides a much better medium for all such containers.

For environmental reasons peat-substitutes, based on other natural materials such as composted bark and re-cycled organic material, as well as plant nutrients, are preferable.

It is important to keep the compost in your containers moist at all times as it is difficult to re-wet if it dries out.

In your local garden centre there will be a wide choice of composts to choose from and if you are not sure which one would be best for your containers, just ask someone for their advice and help.

White Flowers

ARABIS – ROCK CRESS

Annual

Arabis is a mass of bright green foliage with small rosettes of tiny flowers in tufted form. It has similar characteristics as Alyssum.

Plant several together near the edges in containers, window boxes and handing baskets, as they look pretty tumbling down.

6-10 cm height

White only

ARGYRANTHEMUM

Annual

Argyranthemums grow in several varieties colours and sizes to choose from. All of them have large daisy-like flowers, either single or double, and they bloom continuously from early spring to the autumn.

Buy small varieties for containers, window boxes and hanging baskets.

The taller variety look good in clump of 6-8 in a large container.

Up to 65 cm height

Also pink, red, yellow, orange

BACOPA - Snowflake

Annual

Bacopa have tiny white flowers amongst vibrant green leaves which spread and trail and tumble.

It is an excellent plant for the edges of containers, window boxes and hanging baskets.

This plant will flower from April through to the autumn.

10 cm height

Also purple

GYPSOPHILA

Annual

Gypsophila has masses of dense tiny star-shaped flowers on slender stems.

The Alpine variety are very suitable for window boxes and hanging baskets.

The taller varieties look good in containers.

2-15 cm height

Also pale pink

PHLOX

Perennial

Phlox make a wonderful showy addition to summer flowering gardens and there are several varieties and colours to choose from and they are highly-scented.

Choose smaller varieties for window boxes and the centre of hanging baskets. The taller variety look very good in a bunch of 6-8 in a large container.

Up to 60 cm height

Also pink, red, purple

Pink Flowers

DAHLIA

Annual

Dahlias give a bright and long lasting display of many colours and can be bought for various height requirements. Some bloom through the summer, others will bloom late into the autumn.

They need watering well and an occasional feed with a liquid fertilizer.

Smaller varieties are good for containers, window boxes and the centre of hanging baskets.

30-60 cm height

Also white, purple, red, yellow, orange

DIANTHUS

Annual

Dianthus are superb for long lasting summer blooms. They show a mass of multi-coloured flower heads which are clove-scented.

Plant the small variety in window boxes and hanging baskets, while the taller variety, "Sweet William", make a great display if you plant 6-8 plants bunched together in one container.

12-20 cm height

Also white, purple, red, multi-coloured

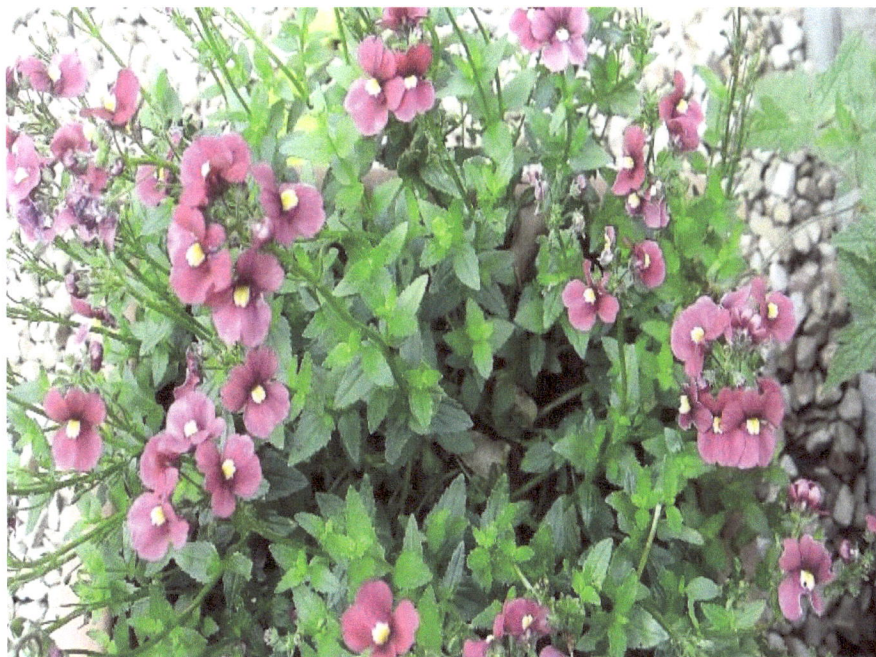

NAMESIA

Annual

Namesia is another great plant for a colourful display throughout the summer. It has many pouched flower heads in a dazzling array of colours. Some varieties are two/three coloured and others are spotted or edged in another colour.

They prefer moist conditions so they should be watered often. Ideal for containers, window boxes and hanging baskets.

20-35 cm height

Also white, red, yellow, orange

PETUNIA

Annual

Petunias are a showy summer plant of funnel-shaped, velvet textured compact or frilly flowers.

They are all ideal for containers, while the trailing varieties are great for window boxes and hanging baskets.

15-35 cm height

Also white, purple, red, yellow

PERSICARIA

Annual

Persicaria are unusual in their very tall and slender long-leafed stalks producing spikes of small funnel shaped flowers.

They spread about during their summer growth so they are best in containers and in the back of window boxes.

25-85 cm height

Also white, red

Purple Flowers

ASTER

Annual

Asters come in many varieties, in many vibrant colours, and in various potential heights.

They make a great display for summer, flowering from May through until autumn.

Buy smaller varieties for containers, window boxes, the middle of hanging baskets.

Water often and carefully.

15-90 cm height

Also white, pink, red, yellow, orange

AUBRETIA

Annual/Perennial

Aubretias are a low carpet-forming plant with abundant small petals, spreading throughout the summer.

They are excellent for the edges of containers, window boxes and hanging baskets.

5-12 cm height

Also in white, pink, red

CAMPANULA

Annual and Perennial

Campanulas, or Canterbury Bells, have wavy-edged hairy leaves with numerous spikes of bell-shaped single, semi-double or double flowerheads.

The dwarf varieties are ideal for containers, window boxes and hanging baskets and it is best to plant the trailing variety at the edges of your containers.

30-45 cm height

Also white, pink, purple

PANSY

Annual/Perennial

Pansies, and their smaller cousins Violas, come in such a choice of varieties and colours it is possible to have them in flower in every month of the year.

All varieties can be grown in containers, window boxes and hanging baskets and water them frequently.

15-24 cm height

Also white, pink ,blue, red, yellow, orange/rusty

STOCKS

Annual

Stocks have grey leaved stems with dense blooms which give off a strong scent of cloves.

Grow in a clump of 3-4 in containers and window boxes.

Up to 75 cm height

Also white, pink, red

Blue Flowers

AGERATUM

Annual

Ageratum are spreading and carpet-forming plants with soft rounded clusters of frothy flower heads.

Grow in containers, window boxes and hanging baskets.

8-12 cm height

Also white, pink

LOBELIA

Annual

Lobelias are a mass of small flowers which spread throughout the summer months.

The trailing varieties are ideal for hanging down over the sides of containers, window boxes and hanging baskets.

10-20 cm height

Also white, purple, red

SCABIOUS

Annual

Scabious have tall and slender near-leafless stalks with a single open pin-cushion flower head.

Small varieties are good for containers and may have to be supported with a bamboo stake if the wind gets up.

30-60 cm height

Also white, pink, purple, yellow

Red Flowers

GERANIUM

Annuals and Perennial

Geraniums come in a vast choice of colours, shapes and habits. Some leaves are variegated, others are furry and many are smooth.

For summer flowering choose compact trailing and spreading sorts.

They provide spectacular colour in containers, window boxes and trailing varieties on the edge of hanging baskets.

Up to 15 cm height

Also white, pink, purple

MIMULUS

Annual

Mimulus is a colourful plant of many vibrant colours set in glossy foliage.

The petals are trumpet shaped, often spotted, and they thrive in a sunny position.

Plant in containers, window boxes and in the centre of hanging baskets.

15-30 cm height

Also yellow, orange

NASTURTIUM

Annual

Nasturtiums give a colourful display of parasol leaves and large velvety trumpet petals.

There is a large selection of colours to choose from - some a single colour and others have a spotted second colour on the petals.

Plant in containers, window boxes and the trailing variety look great when planted on the edge of hanging baskets. The trailing kind may grow through /over/around other plants.

20-60 cm (trailing) height/drop

Also yellow, orange , rust colour

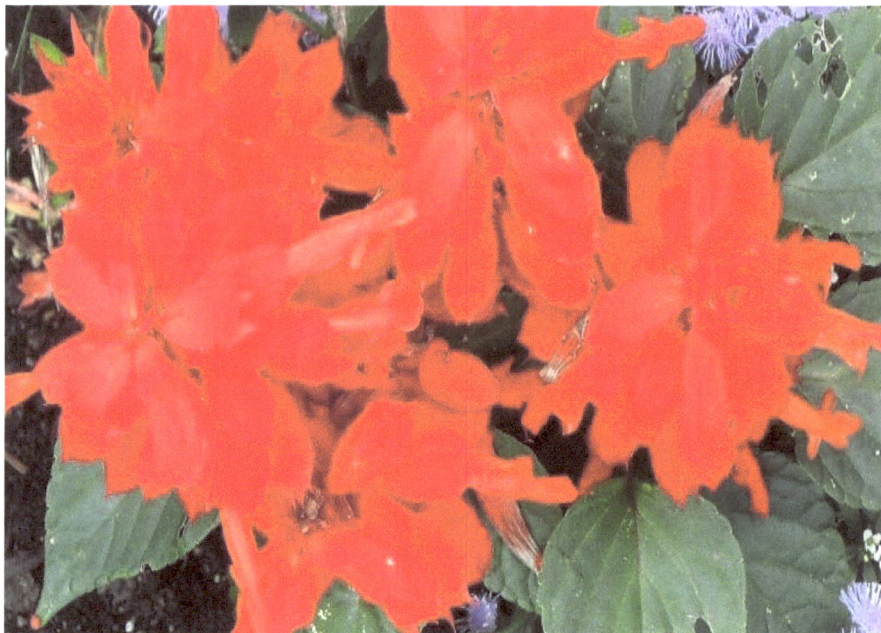

SALVIA

Annual

Salvias can be found in a wide selection of colours and they need to be situated in a sunny and sheltered position.

They give excellent colour in containers, window boxes and the centre of hanging baskets.

15-70 cm height

Also pink, purple, blue yellow

SWEET PEA

Annual

Sweet pea is a rambling/climbing plant with aromatic and multi-coloured petals which will need to be supported as it grows upwards or it can be trailed through/over a fence or trellis.

They can be planted in containers and window boxes, and hanging baskets if they have enough room to tumble over the edges.

Water the plant frequently.

1-2 m height

Also white, pink, purple

Yellow Flowers

BIDENS

Annual/Perennial

Bidens is a trailing free-flowing plant with ferny foliage which is studded with large starry yellow flowerheads.

It is ideal for the edges of containers, window boxes and hanging baskets.

35-50 cm height

BLACK EYED SUSANS

Perennial

Black-eyed-Susans grow tall slim stalks with oval leaves and rich golden yellow flowers with purple-black centres.

They look their best planted in a clump of 6-8 in the centre of a large container situated in a hot spot.

Up to 60 cm height

FRENCH MARIGOLD

Annual

French Marigolds, and also the larger headed African Marigold, are a neat bushy plant with single or double flower heads of orange and yellow supported by dark green separated leaves.

Plant 2-3 together in containers, window boxes and around the edges of hanging baskets.

Beware of slugs as they will easily destroy the whole plant. Water often and well.

10-30 cm height

Also orange, rusty brown

GAILLARDIA – Blanket Flower

Annual

Gaillardia have large open saucer-shaped two-coloured flower heads which provide a highly colourful display from May till at least mid-October. There is a dwarf variety and also those with pom-pom heads.

Plant several together in containers, window boxes and at the edges of hanging baskets. Water well.

30 – 60 cm height

Also pink, red, orange

SUNFLOWER

Annual

Sunflowers may grow to be too big and tall to grow in anything other than a large, and deep, container! There is a more compact variety which is less likely to fall over and the huge flower is easier to see.

You can grow them yourselves from seeds, starting in small containers and progressing to a single large pot for the remainder of its life.

Water well and every day!

The more compact annual variety of sunflower is most often grown as it is less likely to fall over and break and the huge flower is easier to see. The perennial variety has branched flower stems which bear several flower heads. Plant in a single big container or tub or at the very back of a flower bed. It will need to be staked when it reaches about 2 ft. tall.

Up to 2 m height

(Also red, orange)

Orange Flowers

BUSY LIZZIE – IMPATIENS

Annual

Busy Lizzie is one of the most popular plants for summer blooming and requires little maintenance other than watering in dry spells.

There is a wide choice of colours to choose from – including bi-colours of red and white and they all give a showy display from June to early autumn.

They are best grown in containers, window boxes and hanging baskets. Water well.

15-45 cm height

Also white, pink, purple, red

DIASCIA

Annual

Very similar to Nesemia and just as attractive with a mass of open-faced flower heads, in several colours, with contrasting insides.

In bloom from June until early autumn. Ideal for containers, window boxes and hanging baskets.

25-45 cm height

(Also white, pink, purple)

How to choose and plant

Summer blooming plants for containers, window boxes and hanging baskets will be available in your local garden centre from April onwards and come in a wide range of choices.

Most of the plants that you will need to add instant colour to your garden come as tiny plants in cellular plastic packs containing four, six and sometimes a dozen plants.

Plants that come in individual containers are more mature plants (Perennials and Evergreens).

The plants should be compact and have healthy green leaves. Avoid any plants with yellowing foliage as these may have been allowed to get too cold or have been starved of moisture.

Choose plants that are not in full flower as they will not last very much longer so choose plants which have small un-open buds.

The labels on the packs will tell you the name of the plant, where it can be grown, how tall it will become, etc.

Take a look at the labels on the packs as they will often give you further information about how and where to plant.

Pots and Containers

Pots and containers are heavy once they are planted so it is best to plant them up where they are to be displayed. Make sure you choose a container which has drainage holes in the base. Most terracotta pots will have holes but some of the plastic ones do not, so you should make three or four holes in the base before planting. For the best effect choose a container not less than 12" in diameter. I suggest you also buy a corresponding size saucer to go under the pots as this is where you can water the plant as it is the roots that require the moisture.

Cover the drainage holes with stones, gravel or chipped bark to help drainage.

Fill the pot with compost three quarters full and place a tall or bold upright plant in the centre.

Put smaller upright plants around the centre ones and then fill up with more compost to the top of the container.

Finally add trailing plants on the edge so they tumble over.

When the plants are all in, water well and carefully.

Window Boxes

For apartment dwellers window boxes are ideal: they can be placed on a window ledge, fixed to the wall or onto a balcony railing. If you are using a wooden window box it will need to be lined with plastic to prevent the wood rotting. As with pots and containers there should be a few small holes in the base to let air in and for drainage.

If the window box is heavy the plants should be put in when the box is in position. As with pots and containers place a few stones or gravel over the holes in the base to prevent the compost from falling out.

Fill the window box with compost and put taller plants in the middle or at the back if the window box is up against a wall. At the same time you can put some trailing plants over the edges. .

Add smaller upright plants in between the taller plants and the trailing ones.

Water well and remember that if the window box is on a window sill or up against a wall the rain often does not fall into the box so you should water at least once a week to which you could add a liquid feel, such as Baby Bio.

Hanging Baskets

There is a large selection of hanging baskets available in our garden centres. They vary from open-mesh wire baskets to solid-sided wicker/planter ones which will be lined with plastic.

Open-mesh baskets

This kind of hanging basket is the most commonly used but they are also the most difficult to master! It is important to remember that if hanging baskets are hung up quite high it is often only the underneath of them that can be seen so it is best to buy trailing plants for open mesh baskets.

You will need to buy a liner to correspond with the size of the basket. The baskets need to be lined before they can be planted to stop the compost falling out. There are very good liners made from biodegradable 100% natural fibres. Choose a basket of not less than 14" in diameter because the bigger the basket the more compost they will hold and therefore will not dry out too often.

Place the plastic side of the liner upwards in the basket and overlap the segments of the liner in place. Put a few handfuls of compost in the basket and "feed" the roots of trailing plants between the over lapping segments, and into the slits in the liner.

Add more compost and plant further trailing plants through the slits in the liner until they cover the wire mesh when you look at the basket from below. Lastly, add a few upright plants in the centre of the basket. Water the basket carefully with a watering can or gentle hose spray until the water drips out.

Wicker/Willow Baskets & Planters:

Planting in wicker or willow or planters is a lot easier as the base of the basket does not have to be covered – in fact it is attractive to see the wooden part of these baskets. They should come already lined with plastic.

Apart from not using so many trailing plants filling a wicker or willow basket or planter is much the same as filling an open mesh one.

Ideally you should plant a tallish upright plant in the centre, plant a few smaller growing ones around the centre one and if you wish add a few trailers at the edge.

Herbs

Pot Grown Herbs

There are several advantages to growing herbs in a pot particularly in town gardens. (They can also be grown in window boxes which are in a sunny and sheltered position.).

• Herbs require sunshine and well drained compost so by growing them in pots you can move them around to keep them in sunshine.

• Many herbs spread themselves when grown in a flower bed so by growing them in pots the roots are contained.

• In winter time you can bring them inside and keep them on a sunny window sill.

• You can place the pots near the back door to be close by when you need them.

Herbs are best grown in terracotta pots which will absorb the sun's heat and aid the growth although they also absorb moisture so you will need to water them often, especially in warm weather. You will need also to buy a terracotta saucer of corresponding size and when you need to water them put the water in the saucer so that the roots sucks it up. If the pots of herbs are placed beside a fence of wall for shelter rain does not always conveniently fall onto the pots!

You will need to renew the compost in the herb pots each year and to re-pot larger herbs in larger pots, dividing them into two if necessary.

Parsley:

The dwarf-leaved curly variety, as in the photograph, is most often grown and widely used in cooking, but there are also broad-leafed and Italian varieties. Use in salads and for garnishing dishes.

Sage:

There are several varieties of sage. The photograph shows the most usually used and you can also buy red leafed and variegated leafed varieties. All sages have a strong flavour and can be used in stuffing (with onion) for chicken and pork dishes.

Thyme:

Thyme is a part of a large family of perennial herbs, with variegated leaves and a strong flavour. It is very good flavouring to add to stuffing (along with sage) casseroles, soups and all tomato dishes.

Mint:

Mint is a general name for a group of plants which have the aroma and flavour of mint. The leaves may be used fresh or dried but always pick before the plants flower. It can be used in ice cream, or in a summer drink and as a herbal tea.

Chives:

Chives are the smallest (up to 15cm high) of the onion family. Cut them constantly to encourage growth. Use chopped into salads, potato salad, and as a garnish for soups or added to yoghurt or soured cream for a dip.

About the Author

Penelope Murray is a professional gardener who has worked in many gardens in Ireland and the United Kingdom over the past thirty years.

Her speciality is suggesting and planting containers and hanging baskets up in small town gardens, which requires careful planning, as the layout and plants can all be seen from the house and therefore appreciated all year round, usually with little initial outlay and minimum maintenance.

Over the past decade Penelope has developed her own small town garden from the bare patch it was when her house was built in 2002.

Over the same decade, Penelope has also worked in and maintained several larger town gardens, as well as a long-neglected couple of acres in Co. Wicklow.

Presently, Penelope is working on the compilation of a book such as this one which will cover shrubs, evergreens and small trees for containers and she plans a third book for roses and climbers.

www.ingramcontent.com/pod-product-compliance
Lightning Source LLC
LaVergne TN
LVHW010025070426
835509LV00001B/17